I0814903

POLITICAL SYSTEMS IN ACTION

DICTATORSHIP

From Roman Rule to Modern Suppression

ALEX WEBB

Published in 2025 by **Cheriton Children's Books**
1 Bank Drive West, Shrewsbury, Shropshire, SY3 9DJ, UK

First Edition

Author: Alex Webb
Designer: Paul Myerscough
Editor: Sarah Eason
Proofreader: Anna Chambers

Picture credits: Cover: Doodle Press. Inside: p4: Shutterstock/Mohammad Bash, p5: Shutterstock/Elzbieta Sekowska, p6: Wikimedia Commons/Bibliothèque Nationale de France, p8: Shutterstock/Polartern, p9: Shutterstock/Gilmanshin, p10: Wikimedia Commons/Jacques-Louis David, p11: Wikimedia Commons/United States Library of Congress, p12: Shutterstock/Andreas Wolochow, p13: Shutterstock/Igor Golovniov, p14: Alamy/Mccool, p16: Wikimedia Commons/Marcel Antonisse/Anefo, p17: Shutterstock/Cecil Bo Dzwowa, p18: Shutterstock/Alexander Ryabintsev, p21: Shutterstock/Sodel Vladyslav, p22: Shutterstock/Andrew F. Kazmierski, p24: Shutterstock/Everett Collection, p26: Shutterstock/Harold Escalona, p27: Flickr/Xeno_Sapien, p28: Shutterstock/Mansoreh, p29: Shutterstock/Farzad Abdollahi, p31: Wikimedia Commons/Tore Sætre, p32: Shutterstock/Edgar Ortiz, p33: Wikimedia Commons/U.S. Navy/Jesse B. Awalt, p34: Shutterstock/Hung Chung Chih, p35: Wikimedia Commons/Department of Defense, p36: Shutterstock/Gabriel Petrescu, p38: Shutterstock/Mido Semsem, p39: Shutterstock/Dmytro Larin, p40: Shutterstock/Madina Nurmanova, p41: Shutterstock/Emkaplin, p42: Shutterstock/Alexander Khitrov, p43: Shutterstock/LMspencer, p44: Shutterstock/Plavio11.

Printed in the United States of America

Please visit our website,
www.cheritonchildrensbooks.com
to see more of our high-quality books.

Contents

CHAPTER 1

The Story of Dictatorship

In many countries around the world, the president or prime minister is chosen by the people in an election. All adult citizens have a vote and can vote for someone else at the next election if they dislike the way their country is being governed. Millions of people who live in countries ruled by dictatorships have no choice about who leads their country.

Total Power and Control

A dictatorship is a form of government in which one person or a small group of people hold total power. There is no elected body that limits their power and the people they govern cannot vote for a different government at elections. Dictatorships usually seize power by force, particularly during times of national turmoil or emergency, such as during wartime.

Syrians protested on the streets of Aleppo in 2018, calling for an end to the country's civil war, despite the risk of opposing their ruler Bashar al-Assad who was unlikely to back down.

One Group in Charge

Sometimes, a dictator is a single person. However, often absolute power is held by a group such as a political party, which has banned all elections and any other political groups. A dictatorship may also be a combination of the two. Adolf Hitler (1889–1945) was dictator of Germany between 1933 and 1945, but was also leader of the Nazi Party, which formed the country's government.

Political Instability

Dictatorships often arise when a country needs a strong and stable leadership. Adolf Hitler came to power in the 1930s, in part, because Germany was struggling in the aftermath of World War I (1914–1918). The economy was weak, unemployment was high, and the Nazi Party seemed to offer solutions to the country's troubles. Italy, Japan, and Russia also struggled economically, and it wasn't long before dictatorships rose to power there too. Dictatorships promised a way for these countries to regain their former glory. Citizens welcomed a strong leader because it gave them hope that things might change.

Adolf Hitler

DICTATORSHIPS: PAST AND PRESENT

In this book we will look at the political system of dictatorship, its history, and its place in the world today. We'll compare dictatorship past with dictatorship present, and look at some of the key figures of this political system in the People and Politics features. Look out too for the Dictatorship in Action features throughout the book and try to answer the questions that accompany some of them.

An Ancient Beginning

Dictatorship has a long history. Strong, ambitious men, and sometimes women, have always wanted to hold power over others. The first dictatorships, and the first use of the word "dictator," can be found in the ancient world. However, most governments by dictators have been set up in the past 100 years. Why did it take so long for dictatorship to become established?

The First Government

The first government elected by its people ruled the small city-state of Athens in ancient Greece. A form of government in which people have a say in how their country is controlled is known as democracy. Although democracy was established early in Greece's history, it did not spread quickly to the rest of the world. For more than 2,000 years after the birth of democracy in Athens, most rulers around the world were not elected. However, that does not mean that dictators ruled most countries. Many countries were instead ruled by monarchs.

Although kings and queens are not considered dictators, some ruled with strict control and a lack of consideration for their people. This image shows the execution of the French king Louis XVI, who was killed during the French Revolution in 1793. During it, people rose up against the monarchy and rebelled against its grip on France.

Not Dictators

Although kings and queens once often held total power in a country or territory, they were not usually dictators. Rather than seizing power, most monarchs rose to power by being the child of the previous king or, in some cases, by deposing the previous king. In the Christian countries of Europe and elsewhere, people believed that monarchs were chosen by God. For that reason, they were not seen as dictators.

People Having a Say

From the 1800s, the way in which countries were controlled began to rapidly change. Suddenly, people wanted a say in their own government. Many countries were colonies of foreign powers and wanted to rule themselves. As a result, monarchs were overthrown or agreed to work with an elected government. However, if this change of government was marked by unrest and fighting, it was easier for dictators to seize power. During the huge political and social changes of the 1800s, in which revolutions took place and monarchs were overthrown, dictatorships became far more commonplace.

Dictatorship in Action

The German philosopher Oswald Spengler (1880–1936) is believed to have said these words:

> "Either we go to dictatorship in the communist way, or realize that we made a wrong turn and get back to monarchy, culture, realism, and good breeding."

What do you think Spengler meant by "culture" and "good breeding"?

Why do you think Spengler associated dictatorships with communism?

What do monarchs and dictators have in common, and how do they differ? How do these types of rulers come to power? What helps them stay in power?

PAST AND PRESENT:

Are there any monarchs in power today that could be regarded as dictators? Give reasons for your answer.

A Roman Word

The word dictator comes from ancient Rome. The first dictators were very different from our modern-day image of a dictator. Roman dictators were appointed by the Roman senate to lead the city's government during times of crisis. Normally, Roman dictators were allowed to rule only for a period of six months or until the crisis had passed. Power was then removed.

Terror of Tyrants

Our word dictator may have originated in ancient Rome, but the tyrants who ruled some ancient Greek states were more like the modern dictators we know today. Like Roman dictators, tyrants such as Dionysius I of Syracuse seized power during wars and invasions. The ancient Greeks believed a tyrant was anyone who seized power against the laws of the Greek democratic constitution. Since ancient times the word "tyrant" has come to mean any cruel and merciless ruler.

PEOPLE AND POLITICS

Dionysius I of Syracuse (430–367 BCE) was a Greek tyrant who conquered Sicily and parts of southern Italy. During these conquests, he invented the catapult, which became a key weapon in warfare. To help Dionysius maintain total power, he would create distrust among his colleagues. He also had control over his people, because the Syracusans lived in fear that they would be invaded by the Carthaginians, while Dionysius promised to protect them.

Built in the fifth century BCE, the Parthenon in Greece is often regarded as a symbol of democracy, which was founded in Athens during this time. But not all Greek rulers were democratic.

Dictatorship in Action

"If you must break the law, do it to seize power: in all other cases observe it." These words are from the Roman emperor Julius Caesar (100–44 BCE), but they could apply to many dictators. Caesar himself broke the Roman law when he crossed the Rubicon River in Italy and marched his armies toward Rome in 49 BCE, beginning a civil war that would end the Roman Republic, and see the beginning of his rule as a dictator.

Why did Caesar think it was acceptable to break the law to seize power?

Are his words a justification of his actions?

Maybe Caesar believed that he would make Rome a better place by breaking the law? What do you think?

PAST AND PRESENT:

Can you see similar behavior in a modern dictator alive today? Explain your reasons and give examples.

As a dictator, Caesar had almost complete control over the Roman government. During his rule, he carried out several reforms. They included reorganizing the Roman calendar and reforming the tax system. Caesar became so powerful that members of the government feared him, and eventually he was assassinated.

The First Roman Emperor

Following Caesar's death, another dictator, Caesar Augustus, became the first Roman emperor in 27 BCE. He claimed absolute power and set the tone for what was to follow in the Roman Empire—and across the world—for hundreds of years thereafter. Following Augustus' reign, most countries were ruled by monarchs and emperors who passed on power to their children. If an argument took place about whom the next ruler would be, a civil war usually broke out and the winner would then maintain or seize power. Whichever king or queen was in charge, their rule was absolute.

Monarchy Changes

Monarchy power systems began to change in the late 1700s. Britain's colonies in North America declared themselves independent in 1776. These United States declared that they would be ruled by an elected president and congress. Then, in 1789, the people of France overthrew King Louis XVI in a chaotic and very bloody revolution that plunged much of Europe into chaos and war.

PEOPLE AND POLITICS

Napoleon Bonaparte (1769–1821) made himself consul and then emperor of France in 1804, to bring order to the country. Napoleon was able to do this because of his military successes across Europe. Napoleon's many achievements included setting up a legal system that is still used in France today. Although Napoleon held total power and used a network of spies to maintain control over France, his rule shows that dictators are not always bad for their people.

Napoleon Bonaparte

The Story Elsewhere

After Napoleon, dictators took power in many South American countries that had previously been ruled by Spain. Dictators appeared in states in which there was no other government. In 1917, the Russian emperor was overthrown in a revolution, leading to a period of uncertain rule in Russia. Eventually, the Bolshevik Party, led by Vladimir Lenin, took over. This was a new form of dictatorship led by a political group rather than one single person.

Tsar Nicholas II (1868–1918) was leader of Russia until the Bolsheviks overthrew him during the Russian Revolution. The tsar and his family were captured and then eventually killed.

Dictatorship in Action

The ancient Greek philosopher Plato wrote, "Dictatorship naturally arises out of democracy, and the most aggravated form of tyranny and slavery out of the most extreme liberty." Plato also argued that sometimes a wise ruler or small group of rulers, if virtuous and knowledgeable, could govern better than the people.

Are there times when a dictatorship might be seen as a better system of government to live under?

What system of government do you think works best when there are many (perhaps violent) groups competing for control?

Dictatorships have often taken place in countries that were on the verge of becoming democracies. Why do you think this is?

After the War

In the years after World War I, many of the world's most powerful countries were ruled by dictators. World War I was one of the most destructive conflicts in history and caused governments across Europe to fall. Economic problems led many people to feel angry with the leaders who had led them into the war. These disgruntled people were prepared to believe the promises of dictators.

Two Most Powerful

Two of the most powerful dictators to seize power after World War I were Adolf Hitler and Joseph Stalin. Each man was responsible for the deaths of many millions of people. Hitler persecuted the Jews and caused the deaths of millions of people by leading Germany into World War II (1939–1945). Joseph Stalin also murdered millions of people whom he believed were against him.

PEOPLE AND POLITICS

Hitler was one of the first dictators to realize the importance of controlling new media such as radio and movies, as well as traditional forms. Magazine articles portrayed positive images of Hitler, and the year he came to power, an affordable radio was introduced to transmit messages into people's homes. Short news reports were played before feature films, and longer films that promoted the leader and his party's extreme political and social views.

Hitler was a powerful speaker. He persuaded the German people that he had the answers to the problems their country faced.

Backed by Party Power

Hitler and Stalin were both supported by strong party organizations. Hitler's National Socialist Party, also known as the Nazi Party, gained support from the German people when their country faced economic collapse in 1933. The party was democratically elected at first, but then passed laws that meant its power could not be opposed or overthrown.

Rule of Terror

Stalin took over the Bolshevik government established by Lenin in 1924, and set about killing or exiling anyone who could challenge his power. He killed or exiled millions of people. However, Stalin also managed to make the Soviet Union strong enough to withstand Hitler's armies when the German dictator invaded the country during World War II. This was the most horrific war in history and claimed the lives of both Hitler and Italian dictator Mussolini, along with the lives of tens of millions of ordinary people.

Adolf Hitler was often portrayed as a gentle, caring person whom people could relate to.

PEOPLE AND POLITICS

Joseph Stalin (1878–1953) was a dictator who ruled the Soviet Union for nearly one-quarter of a century. He transformed the Soviet Union into an industrial and military superpower, but at the expense of his people. Stalin ruled by terror—anyone who disagreed with his policies was shot, exiled, or sent to a labor camp. He encouraged citizens to spy on each other and he expanded the powers of the secret police to keep track of anyone who might oppose him. Stalin carefully controlled the media to justify his absolute rule.

Joseph Stalin

Didn't Die with Hitler

The idea of dictatorship did not die with Hitler—Stalin remained the leader of the Soviet Union until 1953. The horror of World War II was followed by a period during which the United States and its allies confronted the communist countries led by the Soviet Union. It was also a time in which many new, independent countries broke free from the control of old empires, such as the empires of Britain and France. Conflict and change created opportunities for many new dictators.

Into Eastern Europe

During the Cold War, Stalin and his successors in the Soviet Union provided a lot of military support and money to communist dictatorships in many other parts of the world, particularly Eastern Europe. Even the democratic countries of the West were sometimes prepared to support dictators if they believed that it meant these powerful rulers would then turn away from the Soviet Union, and so help stop the feared spread of communism across the rest of the world.

End of the Soviet Union

Many communist dictatorships in Eastern Europe and worldwide collapsed when the Soviet Union dissolved in 1989. Without the financial and military support once provided by the Soviet Union, the dictatorships that depended upon the support fell apart and were consequently overthrown. However, there are still many countries around the world that are controlled by single dictators or groups of people. They rule with an iron grip and cannot be voted out of power.

Dictatorship in Action

Teodoro Obiang is the longest-serving president in the world, having ruled Equatorial Guinea for more than 45 years. In the 1990s, oil was discovered off the coast of Equatorial Guinea, greatly boosting the country's economy, but for ordinary people, living standards are still poor. In fact, Mbasogo is thought to be one of Africa's most brutal dictators—anyone who opposes his rule is imprisoned or tortured.

Why do you think Obiang holds so much power?

Why do you think the international community hasn't done more to help the people of Equatorial Guinea?

Can you think of other dictatorships in the world today that have been aided by their oil wealth?

CHAPTER 2

Understanding Dictatorship

Dictatorships are not all the same, but they usually share some common features that are explored in this chapter. Some dictators genuinely believe that they can provide good government for a country, and sometimes their people agree. However, in many cases, dictators are more interested in gaining great power and riches for themselves, their friends, and their families.

Robert Mugabe

PEOPLE AND POLITICS

Robert Mugabe (1924–2019) ruled Zimbabwe as president or prime minister for nearly 40 years. When he came to power in 1980, he helped Zimbabwe gain independence after 90 years of British rule. Mugabe oversaw the redistribution of white-controlled land to Black people, and many Zimbabweans considered him to be a hero, but his rule also saw terrible crimes against humanity. Despite severe famine, economic decline, fraud, and extreme violence, Mugabe was reelected many times.

Mugabe's dictatorship finally came to an end when overwhelming opposition to his rule forced him to step down in 2017.

Getting and Keeping Power

Dictatorships are usually focused on how to seize power and how to keep it. They often gain power during a time of conflict and turmoil. To do so they need the support of the nation's army, or a military force large enough to stop the army from overthrowing the dictator. Dictators often begin their careers as military leaders and use the military might they have built up over time to seize control of a country when the time and circumstances allow them to.

Rules Do Not Apply

Dictators believe that the laws that apply to governments and most people in power do not apply to themselves. They will often use tricks and lies to gain power, persuading people that they have only the country's best interests at heart and that they will bring about change that will improve the lives of ordinary people. Once dictators have been voted in or have gained the support of a country's people, they change laws to suit their needs. Remember that dictators often seize power at a time of trouble or turbulence in a country, when it is easier to take control. Once in power, dictators may then hold elections, but they are meaningless because voters are often offered only one candidate to vote for—and that is the dictator!

Dictatorship in Action

Most dictators would not use the word "dictator" to describe themselves. Often, dictators may have taken power with the promise that they will protect a country from an external threat or an inadequate government. Dictators may use a title such as the "Great Liberator" or "Father of the Revolution" to persuade the people that they only seized control to improve their lives. Desperate people are likely to believe the dictator and accept their seizure of power in these situations.

Ancient to Modern

From ancient Rome to the modern Middle East, dictators often come to power promising to restore order. Sometimes, this may be a dictator's actual reason for seizing power. Other times, the dictator may try to convince people of a crisis that does not really exist in order to take control of a country. If the people of a country can be persuaded that they are under threat or that their way of life is threatened, it is far easier to persuade them to allow a new ruler to quickly seize control with the promise of stabilizing the crisis.

The Only Way

Sometimes dictatorship may be the only way to restore order in a country. This is particularly true in a country in which many armed groups are battling for power and endangering and harming the lives of ordinary people. To achieve peace, the dictator must have the support of a military force. Any rebellious force or group that threatens the dictator's absolute control can then be quickly crushed. The dictator may already be in charge of the army. If not, they will ensure that the military leadership is fiercely loyal to them alone.

In China, a strong army helps uphold the firm rule of President Xi Jinping and the Chinese Communist Party.

Not Giving Up

In Roman times, a dictator's rule would last only long enough to restore order, although Julius Caesar is the exception to this rule. However, but modern dictators are not normally ready to give up power so easily. To keep hold of it, they will often try to convince people that the peace and order of their country is continually under threat. They create an atmosphere of intense pressure and a state of fear. Dictators then persuade the people that the only way to maintain stability and order is to keep the dictators in power.

Diverting Attention

If people are preoccupied they are less likely to question what is happening around them. And people's main concern will always be for the safety and wellbeing of themselves and their loved ones. So by deflecting a nation's attention toward a "crisis" or imminent threat happening around them, the dictator can keep his or her iron grip on a country and its people. It is a tactic that works very effectively when any information (such as news from the outside world) that might reveal the truth to people is always blocked.

Dictatorship in Action

Countries are usually at their most united when they are fighting an enemy from outside. Dictators often start conflicts with other nations for this very reason.

Why do you think the idea of a common enemy is useful for a dictator?

How do you think people feel during a time of war?

Can you think of any dictators today who have attacked other countries or groups as a way of uniting their own people?

Help with Hanging On

All dictatorships are different but there are some common methods that most dictatorships rely upon in order to maintain power and control. It is very rare that a dictator can hold on to power entirely on their own. Every dictator needs a group of supporters to help keep them in power. We have already seen that the loyalty of armed forces is important, but dictators usually have a wider group of supporters. In Germany, Nazi leader Adolf Hitler was supported by thousands of members of the Nazi Party, who helped to make his extreme ideas seem reasonable to ordinary people. The supporters also identified and terrorized any people who opposed Hitler. Their fierce support and brutal oppression of anyone who tried to resist Hitler's rule helped the dictator gain and maintain power in Germany.

The Payback Promise

In return for their support, a dictator's helpers are given jobs in government and special privileges. Those rewards might include private houses, great wealth, and the promise of future promotion and power. This system of rewarding supporters helps to ensure their absolute loyalty—as long as the dictator remains in power and as long as no one promises the supporters an even better deal elsewhere!

Dictatorship in Action

In North Korea, three generations of the Kim family have ruled the country for more than 75 years—Kim Il-sung (1912–1994), his son Kim Jong-il (1941–2011), and his grandson Kim Jong-un. Other family members have held key positions in government, helping to justify this rule. However, over the years, there has been dissent within the family. In 2013, Kim Jong-un's uncle was executed as a traitor and in 2017, Kim Jong-un's older half-brother Kim Jong-nam was assassinated.

Why do you think dictators often choose friends and family members to support them?

Why might Kim Jong-un's uncle and half-brother have been seen as a threat to the regime?

No one in the Kim family has stood trial for the assassination of Kim Jong-nam. What do you think this means for other members of the Kim family?

PEOPLE AND POLITICS

Dictators will often create government institutions to give the impression that the country's people have a say in their government. Muammar Gaddafi (1942–2011) ruled Libya, in North Africa, from 1969 to 2011. Although Libya's people were able to vote for representatives in the country's parliament, in reality, Gaddafi retained complete power and control over the country. In 2011, Muammar Gaddafi was finally overthrown when the people rose up.

Muammar Gaddafi

Freedom of Speech

In democratic countries, people are free to say what they like about the government. As long as they stay within the law of the country, people are usually allowed to speak, write, or broadcast freely. In a dictatorship, those who show opposition to the government are restricted in what they can say. In many cases, people can be imprisoned or even killed for daring to criticize a dictator and oppose their vicelike grip on power.

Dictatorship in Action

The Universal Declaration of Human Rights was adopted by the United Nations (UN) in 1948. It includes the following words:

> "Everyone has the right to freedom of opinion and expression; this right includes freedom to hold opinions without interference ... ."

Do you think that you have this right in your country? Can you think of countries and people who do not have these rights?

The UN headquarters in New York City. The UN represents countries of the world to maintain international peace and security, and to promote better living standards and human rights.

No Protection by Law

In most democratic countries law courts protect people from attack or imprisonment by an unjust government. Why doesn't this also happen in a dictatorship? That is because dictators have usually broken the law by seizing power.

Dictators do not recognize sources of power other than themselves —and this includes obeying the law. If a dictator allows people to openly discuss and disagree with their policies, those people might decide to put in place an alternative government and end their dictatorship. For that reason, it is vital that a dictator retains total control over the opinions that people voice.

Watching Words and Actions

In a dictatorship, the government uses many techniques to discover what people are saying and doing, and to control their words and actions. Dictatorship governments are supported by secret police and security organizations that spy on ordinary people. If someone is suspected of being an opponent of the government, action is swift. The suspect may face trial, but there will be little opportunity to defend themself. Often, the suspect will simply disappear, never to be heard of again. With no independent law courts to oppose them, dictators are completely free to act as they choose—and remove anyone who dares to stand against them.

PEOPLE AND POLITICS

In 2016, US university student Otto Warmbier (1994–2017) was visiting North Korea on a guided tour, when he was imprisoned for 15 years for attempting to steal a propaganda poster. Shortly after he was sentenced, Warmbier became very sick and suffered brain damage. He was released 17 months later but died six days after returning to the United States. There were claims that Otto had been tortured before he died.

The US government strongly advises that American citizens do not attempt to visit North Korea due to the risk of arrest and detainment. The government also states that it will not be able to provide emergency help to any citizens in that situation.

Controlling the Media

One way in which dictators can silence their critics is by controlling media such as television, newspapers, and the Internet. Dictators can stop the media from carrying a range of news so that a country's citizens hear only the government's viewpoint. The government can also use media to tell people about their successes, or to even tell lies. This absolute control of information is known as propaganda.

PEOPLE AND POLITICS

Benito Mussolini (1883–1945) was dictator of Italy between 1925 and 1943. Mussolini came to power at a time when his country was in turmoil. As a charismatic leader, he was popular with the Italian people, who thought Italy had been badly treated at the end of World War I, when territories were carved up and Italy gained very little. Propaganda was used to portray an image of Mussolini as a war hero and a leader who would restore order and make Italy great once more.

Benito Mussolini and Adolf Hitler formed an alliance during World War II.

The Power of Propaganda

Adolf Hitler understood the power of propaganda when he became the dictator of Nazi Germany. One of his closest advisors was Minister of Public Enlightenment and Propaganda Josef Goebbels. Goebbels made movies that glorified Hitler and attacked groups such as the Jews, whom the Nazis presented as enemies of Germany. Propaganda helped to convince many Germans that Hitler's hatred of the Jews was justified. Hitler used propaganda to whip up a wave of hatred against German Jews, whom he blamed for the country's economic downfall after World War I. The German Jews were used as scapegoats for the country's many problems, and allowed Hitler to easily deflect public attention away from his vicelike grip on Germany.

Control Today

Dictators today still try to control the media and produce propaganda. Propaganda can include everything from giant posters of the leader on city streets to websites and other online sources that promote government viewpoints. As well as producing propaganda, dictators also control the news that appears on television and in other media, so that people never find out what is really happening in their country.

Dictatorship in Action

In the past, dictators could control everything that was printed or broadcast in a country. The global rise of the Internet since the 1990s has made this very difficult. As a result, dictatorships have often blocked certain sites or tried to prevent people from communicating online altogether.

False online identities can make critics of dictatorship more difficult to track. Why are dictators so afraid of the Internet and the effect it could have on their regimes?

How has the rise of social media changed the way we communicate online? What impact can photographs, videos, and real-time events have on a dictatorship?

PAST AND PRESENT:

With the development of artificial intelligence (AI), how do you think propaganda will change in the future? In what ways does real or fake news help a dictatorship, and in what ways can it be a hindrance?

One Big Cult of Personality

One of the most common uses of propaganda in a dictatorship is to promote the leader's "cult of personality." This is a carefully projected personality that the dictator has created through smart use of media. Dictators want people to believe they are caring, wise, and strong figures. Sometimes dictators are even presented as godlike. Kings and queens first developed the cult of personality. By also presenting themselves as monarchs, dictators try to show people that, like kings and queens, they also have the right to unquestionable rule.

PEOPLE AND POLITICS

Bashar al-Assad took over as president of Syria in 2000 on the death of this father, Hafez, and the al-Assad family has now been in power for more than 50 years. Like his father, Bashar has ruled with a cult of personality. Media campaigns portray him in a glowing light, and even during the devastating civil war that has ravished the country since 2011, propaganda continues to show Bashar in control. People live in fear of criticizing Bashar's government, but some people may believe what they hear because they want it to be true.

Bashar al-Assad

This giant golden statue shows the Turkmenistan dictator Saparmurat Niyazov, and was commissioned by the leader.

An Extreme Example

One of the most extreme cults of personality in recent history was Saparmurat Niyazov (1940–2006), the dictator of Turkmenistan in central Asia. The dictator ordered the creation of a giant revolving statue of himself, which always faced the sun. Cities, a theme park, and even a month of the year were renamed to honor the dictator. Saparmurat Niyazov also wrote a book about Turkmenistan, which was sent to every school in the country to be used as part of the curriculum. The book presented the history of the country as the dictator chose to portray it, with little regard for any historical accuracy.

Dictatorship in Action

Sometimes, a cult of personality is created to focus attention on a single dictator, when, in reality, a group of dictators control a country. In these instances, when a political party or group seizes control of a country, they may build a cult of personality around a single figure. The world's attention is focused on the created personality, while the real power in a country lies elsewhere, such as in the leadership of the armed forces.

Why do dictators spend so much time and money creating a cult of personality? Can you see similarities between this and the way that movie and music stars present themselves to the media?

Celebrities try to stay in the public eye so they can continue their successful careers. Are dictators trying to achieve a similar goal?

PAST AND PRESENT:

Can you think of a modern example of dictatorship that has used the media to create a cult of personality?

CHAPTER 3

Life Under a Dictatorship

When in public, Iranian women wear a hijab as a sign of modesty but also to obey the law.

We have learned how dictators take power and do everything possible to hold on to it. But what do we know about the people who live under a dictatorship? One-third of the world's population, including more than 1 billion people in China, live in countries in which they are unable to choose their leaders. What is life like for them and how does it compare to life for people in a democracy?

Not Always Bad

It would be a mistake to think that dictatorships are always bad for all their people. Although the harsh regime grew to be hated and ended in violence, Muammar Gaddafi's dictatorship in Libya used some of the money it made from selling oil to improve education and living conditions for many of the country's people. Dictators may sometimes also bring peace and stability to a country that is torn apart by civil war. Dictatorships may too provide stability in a country in which there are several violent political groups that could bring about war and bloodshed if they were allowed to attempt to gain control.

Paying a Heavy Price

However, there is often a high price to pay for the stability gained through dictatorship. People in a dictatorship lose many of the rights that are enjoyed by those who live in a democracy. In some dictatorships, people live in constant fear of being arrested or imprisoned without any protection from the law. In the cruellest of dictatorships, millions of people may even lose their lives because of the wishes or prejudices of a dictator. People often count the price of dictatorship for many years after a dictator is no longer in power.

Dictatorship in Action

To understand the experience of living under a dictatorship, consider the things you enjoy in a democracy that you would lose in a dictatorship:

- The right to vote at elections
- The right to speak and write whatever you please
- The right to hold whatever political or religious beliefs you choose
- Protection from independent police and law courts

Do you think these rights are worth having? Which is the most important to you and why?

A picture of Ayatollah Ali Khamenei (right) and Ayatollah Ruhollah Khomeini (left), Iran's first supreme leader.

PEOPLE AND POLITICS

Ayatollah Ali Khamenei has been "supreme leader" of Iran since 1989. He has complete control over the police, who uphold Islamic morals and laws in the country. Women are required by law to wear a hijab (face covering) in public, and surveillance cameras are now used to spot offenders. Punishments have increased with women now facing a fine and up to 10 years in prison, although many women believe wearing the hijab should be a matter of personal choice.

A Collapse of Power

In 1989, many of the communist dictatorships that once held power in Eastern Europe collapsed. Afterward the citizens of East Germany discovered that the Stasi secret police had kept a detailed file for every person. These files now occupy more than 60 miles (97 km) of shelf space. Those who lived through the East German dictatorship can now see their files and how the government was watching every aspect of their lives.

Watched All the Time

People living in dictatorships are used to being watched. Security cameras watch the streets. People's neighbors, or even other family members, may be forced to spy on them. Any small sign of opposition to the dictatorship, even just a few careless words, could mean a person loses their job or is interrogated or imprisoned without hope of trial.

Killed for Taking a Stand

In the most extreme dictatorships, thousands of people may even be murdered simply for disagreeing with the dictatorship. Suspects can be tortured to gain information. In a country in which the only law is that of the dictator, ordinary people have no protection at all and live in constant fear for their lives.

People Who Try to Help

While the people living under a dictatorship have little chance to protest, international human rights organizations, such as Human Rights Watch and Amnesty International, will often campaign for the release of political prisoners. These important organizations are constantly raising awareness of the plight of people who are wrongly imprisoned under the world's extreme dictatorships.

Dictatorship in Action

In the following extract, a former East German citizen explains the impact that constant spying by security forces has had on her life.

> "The stories are always in the back of my head whether I'm lying in bed or out in social situations. I find it hard to trust people."

Can you think of other ways that people's lives might be affected long after they stop living in a dictatorship?

PAST AND PRESENT:

Can you think of some examples of modern spying that have affected people living under a dictatorship?

Yeonmi Park

Yeonmi Park is regarded as one of the most famous North Korean defectors. She fled the totalitarian regime in 2007 at the age of 13, traveling first to China and then to South Korea and the United States. Park's accounts of the North Korean regime are detailed in her book *In Order to Live*. Her interviews and videos have gone viral, telling us much about life under the dictatorship, including harsh punishments and the devastating effects of the North Korean famine. But inconsistencies in these stories have led many to question the exact truth of Park's words.

Especially Difficult for Some

Life can often be especially difficult for particular groups of a population living under a dictatorship. We have seen that one method dictators often use to unite their people is to find a convenient enemy, often within their country. Saddam Hussein persecuted the Kurdish minority living in the north of Iraq, and even used chemical weapons against them. Probably the most catastrophic example of this type of persecution was Hitler's devastating treatment of the Jews.

People Under Attack

Hitler often attacked the Jews in his early speeches as he sought to gain control of Germany. After the dictator came to power in 1933, he began to persecute Jewish businesses. Jews were stripped of their rights as German citizens. Other groups Hitler attacked included Roma people and homosexuals. During World War II, Hitler and his supporters began to murder vast numbers of Jews. It is believed 6 million of the 9.5 million Jews who had lived in Europe before World War II were murdered during Hitler's regime. This mass murder of the Jews is known as the Holocaust.

Auschwitz was a concentration camp in Poland during World War II. By 1944, the camp held over 9,000 Jews, as well as nearly 4,000 Poles and almost 3,000 prisoners of other ethnicities.

Omar al-Bashir

PEOPLE AND POLITICS

The Holocaust is one of the most horrific crimes in history, yet similar atrocities have happened in recent years, too. Omar al-Bashir was a dictator in Sudan for 30 years. He came to power in 1989 after leading a military coup and used force to hold onto power until he was finally ousted in a coup in 2019. Al-Bashir was imprisoned for corruption and for leading the 1989 coup. He has been accused of war crimes, including allowing the murder of thousands of civilians in the Darfur region of Sudan.

Dictatorship in Action

The information you have discovered about dictatorships should help you to understand how something as terrible as the Holocaust could happen. The Jews were a distinct group in German society. This helped Hitler to single them out and blame them for Germany's problems. Other important factors that lead to the persecution of a group of people within a dictatorship include:

- The dictatorship's control of the media
- People's fear of opposing a brutal regime that could easily arrest and imprison them
- The cult of personality built around a dictator such as Adolf Hitler

All these things help to explain why ordinary people did not prevent the terrible crimes against the Jews from taking place in Nazi Germany.

CHAPTER 4

Pushing Back against Dictatorship

It can be extremely difficult for people to fight back against a dictatorship because ordinary people within an oppressive regime have so little power. Thankfully, many of history's dictatorships did eventually come to an end. Some of them ended in violence, others ended when the dictator allowed a gradual transition toward democracy. However, dictatorships still exist around the world.

Death and Survival of Dictatorships

Dictators may spend a lot of time and effort convincing people that they are all-powerful, but eventually all dictators grow old and die. Sometimes, the dictator's government dies with them, but other times, family members succeed power and the dictatorship continues under their rigid control.

PEOPLE AND POLITICS

Mao Zedong (1893–1976) was China's first communist leader. During his rule, policies such as the Great Leap Forward (1958–1961) and the Cultural Revolution (1966–1976), tried to make China great again after what was regarded as a "Century of Humiliation." Mao's policies didn't always have the desired effect, however, and China suffered famine and economic uncertainty. Subsequent leaders brought their own policies and style to communist China.

A statue of Mao Zedong

Able to Hang On in China

Some dictatorships can endure because in these regimes power is not held by one single person. The current government of China is such a dictatorship—its people cannot vote against it and criticism of the government is not allowed. The Chinese government has held power since 1949. That is because, since the death of its founder Mao Zedong, the government has not depended on the power and personality of just one single leader to ensure the survival of China's long-lasting dictatorship.

Promoting Peace and Security

The UN is an organization made up of nearly all the countries on Earth. One of its goals is to promote peace and security around the world, and protect human rights. The organization has certain powers, including the right to impose sanctions to stop other countries trading with dictators. In extreme cases, the UN may allow countries to take military action against a dictatorship. This happened when international troops forced Saddam Hussein's Iraqi army to end its invasion of Kuwait in 1991.

Dictatorship in Action

Saddam Hussein (1937–2006) was able to stay in power in Iraq for more than 20 years by combining a brutal regime with a series of wars against his country's neighbors. The dictator was swept from power by US-led forces in 2003.

Why do you think Saddam chose to defy the international community in a way that led to his downfall?

PAST AND PRESENT:

Can you compare Saddam Hussein with a more recent example of dictatorship and a dictator who has created a cult of personality?

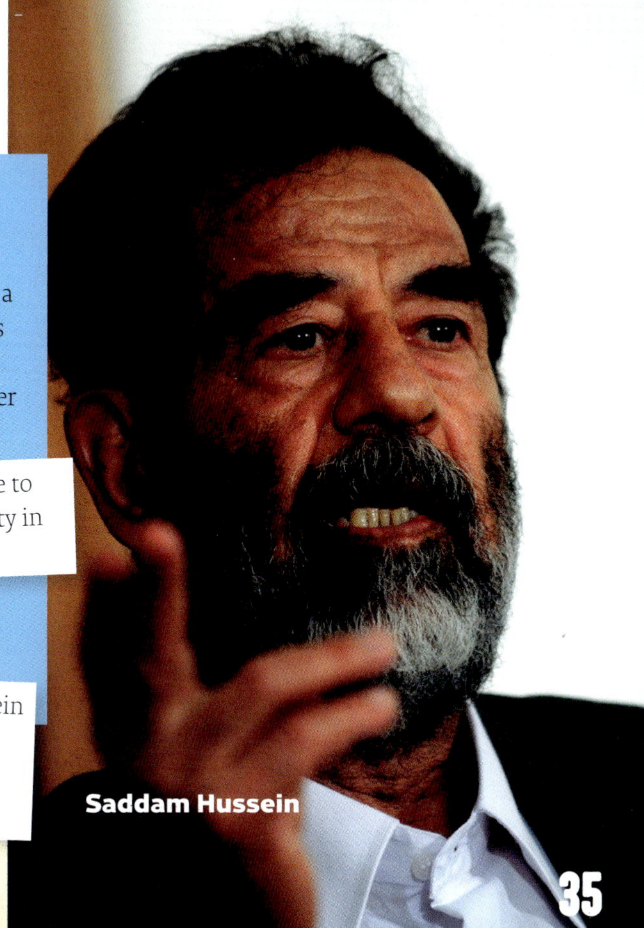

Saddam Hussein

Building Support

Dictators survive by building a state apparatus that supports them and prevents others from challenging them. They restrict access to the media so different points of view cannot be expressed. They in turn control the information that people do have access to, supplying them with a constant stream of propaganda. Dictatorships imprison and even kill those who disagree with them. However, well-organized opposition can often triumph over dictators. How is this achieved?

Built on Shaky Foundations

One reason why dictatorships spend so much time showing how strong they are is because they know that their power may be based on shaky foundations. A dictator may have only a very small group of supporters, especially when they are compared to the population of a country.

In 1989, the people of Romania demonstrated against their dictator Nicolae Ceaușescu. The dictator used his army to attack the protestors but the demonstrations just became bigger and bigger, until Ceaușescu was eventually forced from power.

PEOPLE AND POLITICS

Nicolae Ceauşescu (1918–1989) was a dictator in Romania from 1965 until 1989, when he was overthrown and killed in a revolution. Ceauşescu used a cult of personality to hold onto power, as well as controlling the media, appointing family members to important government positions, and using secret police to find opposition to his rule. In an attempt to increase Romania's population, women were obliged to have at least five children, but Ceauşescu's policies led to many unwanted orphans in the country.

Wave of Protest

Protests that overthrow dictatorship can be triggered by a number of situations. Sometimes they are a response to changes in another country. This was the case when waves of protests swept the Arab World in 2010–2011 (see page 38). These protests began in Tunisia where the government fell, encouraging protests in neighboring countries, too. However, in some cases the opposition was met with increased force. Sometimes, the government can trigger rebellion, for example, by arresting an opponent and infuriating the country's people so much that they rise up against the regime. Sometimes, the trigger might be an issue such as high food prices.

Trained to Follow Orders

Dictators always depend on the loyalty of the armed forces, which are normally more heavily armed than ordinary citizens. Military personnel are trained to follow orders, but they also endure life under a harsh dictatorship. When a large part of the armed forces decides to switch sides and supports the opposition dictatorships are threatened.

A switch of sides took place in Gabon in 2023 when a military coup ended the Bongo family's 55-year rule. The military placed the dictator Omar Bongo under house arrest and then took control of the country. Crowds took to the streets to celebrate the end of the long-lasting dictatorship.

Nicolae Ceaușescu and his wife Elena were executed in 1989 for economic sabotage and crimes against humanity. Despite Ceaușescu's crimes, some people do not believe the ruler was a dictator and still visit his grave to commemorate his birthday.

Protests in Egypt in 2013 led to the overthrow of President Morsi, but despite elections, his successor Abel Fattah al-Sisi, continues to govern with authoritarian rule.

Standing Firm

In December 2010, a protest by a street vendor in Tunisia triggered a series of rebellions against dictatorship across North Africa and the Arab world, known as the "Arab Spring." Some of the rebellions were successful, others were ended with brute force. A decade later in another part of the world, the people of Ukraine fiercely resisted Russia's invasion of their country. That fierce resistance is still ongoing today. Despite the dangers of opposing a dictator, history has shown that people can find the strength to stand up for what they believe is right and stand firm against ruthless dictatorships.

Mixed Reaction

The Arab Spring protests began in Tunisia, where they successfully overthrew the government. After 23 years of authoritarian rule, the country went on to build a democracy with free and fair elections. However, the effects of the COVID-19 pandemic badly damaged Tunisia's economy and authoritarian measures have returned to the country again. Elsewhere, the Arab Spring protests were met with immediate opposition. In Bahrain, for example, the protests were brutally suppressed, with help from troops of neighboring country Saudi Arabia, and in Syria, Bashar al-Assad refused to back down, unleashing death, destruction, and civil war on the people he claimed to lead. Syria is still under Assad's iron-grip control.

Brave Resistance

In February 2022, when thousands of Russian troops invaded Ukraine, the United States offered to evacuate the Ukrainian president Volodymyr Zelenskyy and his family. But Zelenskyy stood firm. Despite facing the wrath of a world superpower, under the dictatorship of Vladimir Putin, Zelenskyy and the Ukrainian people fiercely resisted. Zelenskyy used social media and live broadcasts to rally his troops and empower his citizens, and pleaded to world leaders to help Ukraine in their fight. In the early days of the war, the international community were skeptical of a small nation being able to resist Russia's aggression, but Ukraine defied the odds. And after years of war, despite exhaustion, they are not giving up the fight.

Dictatorship in Action

In 2022, Ukrainian president Volodymyr Zelenskyy was addressing an audience at the Cannes Film Festival and quoted the words of Charlie Chaplin:

> "The hate of men will pass, and dictators die, and the power they took from the people will return to the people. And so long as men die, liberty will never perish."

This quote comes from the final scenes of Charlie Chaplin's movie *The Great Dictator* (1940), a comedy about a Hitlerlike dictator, with serious undertones about authoritarian rule.

Why do you think Zelenskyy chose to talk at a film festival?

What roles have films played in supporting dictators but also opposing them?

What is the "power" that Charlie Chaplin refers to?

Volodymyr Zelenskyy

CHAPTER 5

The Future of Dictatorship

Dictators face many forces that make it difficult for them to hold onto power, but there are still many dictatorships in place around the world. Although they appear to control power, dictators are as vulnerable to economic forces as other governments. For example, dictatorships are particularly vulnerable to the rising price of food. When people cannot afford food, they have less to lose by attacking their leaders.

A Difficult Place for Dictators

The end of the Cold War (1947–1991) has made the world a more difficult place for dictators. The Soviet Union helped to support dictatorships in Eastern Europe and elsewhere. Today, dictators have fewer allies as they try to hold on to power. Fidel Castro (1926–2016) was dictator in Cuba for almost 50 years before handing over power to his brother, Raul. For much of that time, Castro depended on support from the Soviet Union. The end of that vital support has forced the Cuban regime to adapt and change.

Vladimir Putin has kept control of Russia since 1999.

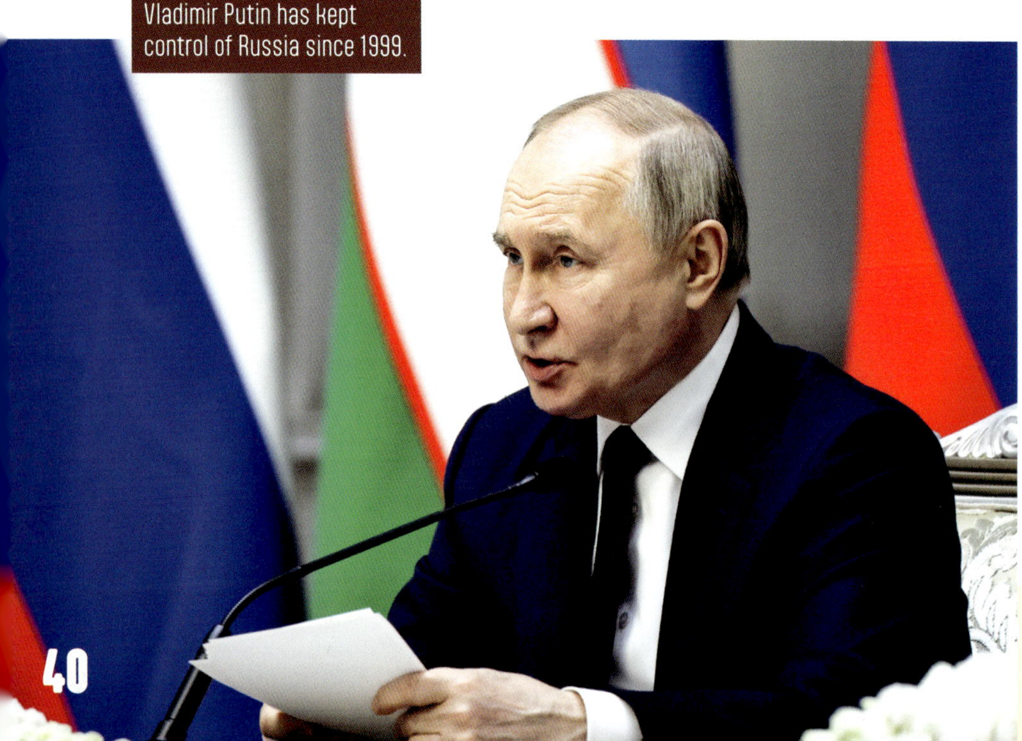

Dictatorship Still Possible

Despite significant global changes, there are still dictators in many countries around the world. Also in power are leaders who claim to be democratic, but run unfair elections to make sure they are never voted out. For example, in 2024, Vladimir Putin was reelected for a sixth term in office, but faced no serious opposition during the electoral process. New dictatorships are also taking control of some areas of the world, where uncertainty and upheaval make it easy for dictators to move in. In Venezuela, for example, economic collapse is sowing the seeds of more authoritarian rule.

Dictatorship in Action

Today, around two-thirds of the world's people are online and social media is helping to spread messages across the globe faster than ever before in our history.

Do you think our online world is likely to help dictators or make life more difficult for them?

In what ways could dictators use the Internet and social media to spread their own ideas?

What impact do you think banning Internet use has on our perceptions of a country?

Fidel Castro took power in Cuba after a revolution in 1959. He introduced communism to the country and vowed to improve education and healthcare. During the Cold War, Cuba was closely allied with the Soviet Union which gave it economic support but also led to sanctions from the United States. When the Soviet Union collapsed, Cuba faced economic uncertainty and a renewed need to justify its communist rule. Castro tried to garner the support of his people in the country's decision-making to strengthen his rule.

Fidel Castro

A Hidden Dictator

No one knew much about North Korea's new leader Kim Jong-un when he took power in 2011. Information about his life had been kept secret. What the public did know was that he was the youngest son of Kim Jong-il, who held power for 17 years. He succeeded his own father Kim Il-sung who had ruled since establishing North Korea's communist government, named the Democratic People's Republic of Korea (DPRK) in 1948. For more than 75 years, three generations of the Kim family have been the dictators of North Korea.

PEOPLE AND POLITICS

When his father died in 2011, Kim Jong-un became one of the world's youngest leaders at the age of 27. His older brothers had fallen out of favor with the family, or were thought unsuitable to govern. Although there was uncertainty about Jong-un's ability to rule at such a young age, he was quick to consolidate his position and take control. He appointed close advisors and family members to key government positions. While living standards in North Korea have improved under his leadership, a combination of international sanctions and the challenges of the COVID-19 pandemic have had a devastating effect on the economy and food supplies.

Kim Jong-un

North Koreans are encouraged to see their leaders as positive and inspiring. These statues show former leaders Kim Il-sung and Kim Jong-il.

Ruling with an Iron Fist

Since gaining power, the Kims have imposed a strict regime in the country. Information is tightly controlled—both coming into and out of the country. Cell phones can be used, but not to call other countries. The media is censored, too. The Internet is very different in North Korea. Users can only visit government-approved sites that include chat functions, and media sponsored by the government. People who speak against the government can be sent to prison camps. These are harsh labor camps where many die from bad working conditions and malnutrition.

Dictatorship in Action

North Korea's unique isolationism is one factor that has helped the Kim dictatorship to survive. Cultural isolation has made it easier for the government to keep control because citizens don't know what life is like "on the other side." Similarly, the international community cannot know for certain what goes on inside the country's borders. But isolationism also can cause difficulties with the economy, and with food and medical supplies.

Why do you think North Korea chose to isolate itself from the rest of the world?

What benefits do you think North Korea might gain from building relationships with other nations? Could these new relationships be a threat to the regime?

PAST AND PRESENT:

With globalization, the world is becoming an increasingly small place. Do you think North Korea will be able to stay isolated in the years ahead?

CONCLUSION

Dictatorships Past, Present, and Future

Throughout this book, we have learned that dictatorships take many forms. We know that they have existed since ancient times, with the general Julius Caesar becoming one of the first Roman dictators. Most of the world's dictators have ruled since 1900, using mass communication and military strength to support their governments. Some dictators, such as Adolf Hitler and Joseph Stalin, are responsible for mass murder on a truly horrifying scale.

Vladimir Putin (left) and Xi Jinping (right) have both made changes to their country's constitution in recent years, to ensure the longevity of their rule.

What It Takes to Stay on Top

We have discovered how dictators gain and keep power. We know how they manipulate the media and use propaganda to convince people that dictatorship is best for them. We have also learned that, as the Romans knew, strong leadership can be a good thing in times of crisis. However, too often dictators are focused only on keeping their own power, while ignoring the rights and wishes of the people they lead. We have discovered how people can fight back against dictators, even if they have no political voice.

Still a Way to Go

Although the twentieth century saw the fall of many long-serving dictators, from Muammar Gaddafi to Saddam Hussein, the issue of great economic uncertainty in the twenty-first century has seen a rise of authoritarian rule in many nations. And in an increasingly online world, citizens are becoming more educated and politically informed, presenting a challenge to dictators, but in some countries dissent has been overruled with an iron fist. Dictators such as Vladimir Putin and Bashar al-Assad seem to have no intention of backing down and ending their dictatorships.

Changing the Rules

In recent years, some dictators have changed the rules to ensure that they remain in power. In 2018, for example, President Xi Jinping amended China's constitution to abolish two-term limits to his presidency, effectively meaning he could rule for life. Similarly, in 2021, Russian president Vladimir Putin passed a law that could keep him in office until 2036. The question is, will dictatorships such as this survive into the future or is the era of dictatorships marked?

Dictatorship in Action

Lawyer and 1940 Republican presidential nominee Wendell Willkie (1892–1944) once said:

> "It is from weakness that people reach for dictators and concentrated government power. Only the strong can be free. And only the productive can be strong."

What does this quote tell us about the advantages and disadvantages of dictatorship?

What world conditions affect the political choices that a government makes?

How can we help to make the world a better place, so that forms of government work for the good of ordinary citizens as well as for the good of the country as a whole?

Glossary

absolute power government in which no challenge to authority is allowed

allies countries that stand together in a fight against something

citizens members of a country

civil war an internal conflict between two, or more, groups in a country

colony a country that is ruled over by another country, as part of an empire

communist a system of government where the state controls all wealth and property

concentration camp a prison camp where large groups of people are imprisoned, usually without having been convicted of a crime

congress the group of people who are elected to help govern the United States

constitution a set of rules and principles that lays down how a nation should be governed

consul a senior elected officer of a government, first used in ancient Roman republics

democracy a system in which the government is voted for by most or all the adults in that country

deposing forcing to leave power

dictatorship government by a leader who rules with absolute power

emperor a monarch who rules over an empire

exiling forcing a person to leave a country

Holocaust the organized murder of millions of Jews, and other groups, before and during World War II

human rights rights that every human being has, regardless of their race, sex, or religion

informants people who pass information about other people to an institution

institutions organizations created for professional, social, educational, or religious purposes

interrogated questioned harshly

mass media means of communication that can reach large numbers of people, such as radio or television broadcasts

monarch a king or queen, who rules in a monarchy

oppressive controlling with force

persecuted treated harshly, or singled out for harsh treatment

police security officers who maintain security within a country, particularly in secretive or repressive governments

political party a group of people with similar ideas about how a country should be run

propaganda the spreading of information to influence public opinion or present the person creating the information in a favorable way

reform political or social change

regime a controlling state
Roma a group of traveling people who originally came from Asia, but are now found across the world
sanctions laws that prevent a country from buying goods from, or selling them to, other countries
Soviet Union a union of countries in Eastern Europe, led by Russia, which lasted until 1991
suppressed kept down
suspect a person believed to be guilty of doing something wrong
United Nations (UN) an organization that includes representatives of most countries in the world, and that rules in cases of international disputes

Find Out More

Books

Butler, Denice. *Dictatorship: Authoritarian Rule* (Systems of Government). Mason Crest, 2018.

Portus, Sam. *Fascism: Radical Nationalism* (Systems of Government). Mason Crest, 2018.

Uhl, Xina M. *Dictatorship* (Examining Political Systems). Rosen, 2020.

Websites

Take a closer look at dictatorships around the world at:
https://academickids.com/encyclopedia/index.php/Dictatorship

Discover more about autocratic power at:
https://education.nationalgeographic.org/resource/autocracy

Find out more about the history of dictatorships at:
https://people.howstuffworks.com/dictator2.htm

Publisher's note to educators and parents:
All the websites featured above have been carefully reviewed to ensure that they are suitable for students. However, many websites change often, and we cannot guarantee that a site's future contents will continue to meet our high standards of educational value. Please be advised that students should be closely monitored whenever they access the Internet.

Index

ABOUT THE AUTHOR

Alex Webb has written many children's books and has a particular interest in history and politics. She has found researching and writing this book fascinating and hopes that it helps students everywhere gain knowledge and insight into political systems and how they work.